Walford's History of
NEWINGTON & WALWORTH

LOCAL HISTORY REPRINTS
316 Green Lane, Streatham, London SW16 3AS
Telephone 0181-677 9562

Originally published in 1872-78 by
Cassell and Company Limited
as part of
Old and New London
by
Edward Walford M.A.

This edition published in 1996 by
Local History Reprints
316 Green Lane
Streatham
London SW16 3AS

ISBN 1 85699 058 3

INTRODUCTION

Edward Walford was born at Hatfield Place, near Chelmsford, on 3rd February 1823. His family roots were well and truly planted in the Church, his father, the Revd William Walford, being the Rector of St. Runwald's Church, Colchester, and his mother, Mary Ann Walford, being the daughter of the Revd Henry Hutton, Rector of Beaumont in Essex, and chaplain of Guy's Hospital.

As befitted a clergyman's son he attended the Church of England school at Hackney, where he was tutored by Edward Churton, later to become archdeacon of Cleveland. After this he went to Charterhouse, one of England's finest public schools which was then under the headship of Augustus Page Saunders, later to become dean of Peterborough.

Edward was a gifted scholar, and matriculated from Balliol College, Oxford in 1841. In 1843 he won the chancellor's prize for Latin verse, and graduated B.A. in 1845 and M.A. two years later in 1847. Not surprisingly, given his family background and education, he was ordained as a deacon in 1846, becoming a priest in the following year. His flair for learning continued and he was successful in winning the Denyer theological prize in both 1847 and 1848.

His early career was pursued in the world of education. His first post in 1846 was that of assistant-master at Tonbridge school. This was followed from 1847-1850 by a period as a private tutor when he prepared pupils in both London and Clifton for entry to Oxford.

Edward met his first wife, Mary Holmes, whilst teaching in Clifton in 1847, and by her had a daughter, Mary Louisa. In February 1852 he married for a second time when he took as his bride Julia Talbot, the daughter of Admiral Sir John Talbot.

In the 1850's Walford's career moved more and more towards writing and he had several books published including a "Handbook on the Greek Drama". In June 1858 he became the editor of the "Court Circular", however this was not a successful venture, and a year later he withdrew from the position after losing £500 in the venture. This early set back did not appear to dampen his enthusiasm, and from 1859 to 1865 he was connected with the periodical "Once a Week" first as sub-editor, and afterwards as editor. This was followed by a period of almost 30 months as editor of the famous "Gentleman's Magazine" which he left in May 1868 when the publication came under new management.

His editorial duties did not prevent Edward from writing, and he produced a series of biographical and genealogical publications including "Records of the Great and Noble" in 1857, "County Families of Great Britain" in 1860 and "Life of the Prince Consort" in 1861. His publication of cheap reference works such as "Hardwicke's Shilling Baronetage and Knightage," "Hardwicke's Shilling Peerage," and "Hardwicke's Shilling House of Commons" gained him a reputation as a popular writer of his day.

Walford is best remembered today for his topographical books on London. Following the death of George Thornbury in 1876, Edward continued the major Victorian history of our capital city which Thornbury had started in 1872, completing the last four of the six volumes of "Old and New London" in 1878. It is from volume 6 of "Old and New London" that this reprint of the chapter on Newington and Walworth is taken.

In 1879 Walford published a further two volumes on London called "Londoniana". His trio of major works on London was completed in 1883-4 when he published two volumes entitled "Greater London". This publication adopted the same format as "Old and New London" and dealt with the history of London's rapidly expanding outer suburbs. Walford's London books drew heavily from the writings of other popular antiquaries of his day, such as John Timbs and Peter Cunningham, none the less it is true to say that the eight volumes of "Old and New London" and "Greater London" provided the standard reference work on the capital for generations of Londoners.

Surprisingly no history of London of similar size or popular appeal was published for more than half a century after Walford's works, which is a fitting testimonial to his labours. Edward died at Ventnor on the Isle of Wight on 20th November 1897.

JOHN W BROWN

London as it was and as it is.

WRITING the history of a vast city like London is like writing a history of the ocean—the area is so vast, its inhabitants are so multifarious, the treasures that lie in its depths so countless. What aspect of the great chameleon city shall one select? for, as Boswell, with more than his usual sense, once remarked, "London is to the politician merely a seat of government, to the grazier a cattle market, to the merchant a huge exchange, to the dramatic enthusiast a congeries of theatres, to the man of pleasure an assemblage of taverns." If we follow one path alone, we must neglect other roads equally important; let us, then, consider the metropolis as a whole, for, as Johnson's friend well says, "the intellectual man is struck with London as comprehending the whole of human life in all its variety, the contemplation of which is inexhaustible." In histories, in biographies, in scientific records, and in chronicles of the past, however humble, let us gather materials for a record of the great and the wise, the base and the noble, the odd and the witty, who have inhabited London and left their names upon its walls. Wherever the glimmer of the cross of St. Paul's can be seen, we shall wander from street to alley, from alley to street, noting almost every event of interest that has taken place there since London became a city.

OLD AND NEW LONDON

A NARRATIVE OF

Its History, its People, and its Places

Illustrated with numerous Engravings from the most Authentic Sources

THE SOUTHERN SUBURBS

BY

EDWARD WALFORD, M.A.

POPULAR EDITION

Vol. VI

CASSELL AND COMPANY, Limited
LONDON, PARIS & MELBOURNE

NEWINGTON AND WALWORTH.

"Utrum rus an urbem appellem, prorsus hæreo."—*Plautus.*

Etymology of Newington Butts—The "Elephant and Castle"—Joanna Southcott—Singular Discovery of Human Remains—The Drapers' Almshouses—The Fishmongers' Almshouses—Newington Grammar School—Hospital of Our Lady and St. Catherine—Newington Theatre—The Semaphore Telegraph—The Metropolitan Tabernacle—Mr. C. H. Spurgeon—Mr. Spurgeon's Almshouses and Schools—St. Mary's Church, Newington—The Old Parish Church—The Graveyard laid out as a Public Garden—The Clock Tower—The Old Parsonage House—The "Queen's Head" Tea Gardens—A Great Flood—An Eminent Optician—The Surrey Zoological Gardens—The Music Hall—Walworth Road—Carter Street Lecture Hall—The Walworth Literary and Mechanics' Institution—St. Peter's Church—St. John's Church.

NEWINGTON is within the limits of the parliamentary borough of Lambeth; it is a parish of itself, and adjoins Southwark on the south. It was anciently called Neweton, or New Town. Lysons considers that in early times the church of this parish stood at Walworth, and that on its removal further westward, the buildings erected around it gradually acquired the name of "the New Town."

A small portion of the main road through the parish, running southward from the "Elephant and Castle," is called Newington Butts, which, writes Northouck, is thought to have been so designated, "from the exercise of shooting at the butts which was practised there, as in other parts of the kingdom, to train the young men in archery." Other writers, however, are of opinion that the derivation is from the family of Butts, or Buts, who owned an estate here.

The "Elephant and Castle" public-house, now a mere central starting-point for omnibuses, was formerly a well-known coaching house; its sign was the crest of the Cutlers' Company, into whose trade ivory enters largely.

This celebrated tavern is situated about one mile and a half from Westminster, Waterloo, and Blackfriars Bridges, and on a spot where several cross roads meet, leading from these bridges to important places in Kent and Surrey. Before railways drove our old stage-coaches from the road, the "Elephant and Castle" was a well-known locality to every traveller going anywhere south of London. Its character, however, has become to a certain extent changed, and it is now chiefly known to the inhabitants of Camberwell, Dulwich, Herne Hill, Kennington, Stockwell, and Clapham.

In the Middle Ages, as we are reminded by Mr. Larwood, in his " History of Signs," the elephant was nearly always represented with a castle on his back. Early manuscripts represent the noble brute with a tower strapped on his back, in which are seen five knights in chain armour, with swords, battle-axes, cross-bows, and emblazoned shields, thus realising the words of the Roman satirist, Juvenal—

"Partem aliquam belli et euntem in prælia turrim."

The " castle," in elaborate and costly sets of chessmen, is often set on the back of an " elephant."

In the early part of the present century this spot had an additional renown. Within a few doors of the old inn, Joanna Southcott, of whom we have spoken in our notice of St. John's Wood,* set up a meeting-house for her deluded followers. Her disciple, Mr. Carpenter, covered the walls with strange pictures representing, as he said, visions

THE TELEGRAPH TOWER, IN 1810.

he had received; "thousands of delusionists." observes a writer in the *Dispatch*, " visited the chapel, and prayed that old Joanna might speedily be delivered of the expected Shiloh. But though a silver cradle was subscribed for and presented. Nature refused to work a miracle, and no Shiloh came. After a time, Joanna and her friend Carpenter quarrelled. The old woman retired with

---

* See Vol. V., p. 253.

another disciple, Mr. Tozer, to Duke Street, Lambeth, and there built another chapel, leaving Carpenter in possession of the Newington house. What he preached there we know not; but in fulness of time Joanna died, and then numbers awoke to the delusion, and wondered how they could have believed in the divine mission of the ignorant, quarrelsome old woman."

In 1875, whilst some workmen were engaged in laying down pipes for the water company, a portion of the roadway in front of the "Elephant and Castle," and within a few feet of the kerb, was opened, when one of the men came upon what he thought at first was a box, but what in the end proved to be a coffin containing human remains. These were found to be those of a person, it was believed, of some sixteen years of age. All the parts were nearly complete, but, singular to state, there was an absence of either hands or feet. The skull was in a wonderful state of preservation, but on one side there was an indentation, as though a blow had been given causing a fracture. In the coffin was found a clasp-knife, somewhat resembling that carried by sailors. There was also a piece of woollen fabric, upon which were marks believed to be those of blood. The discovery was considered as very singular, considering the frequent alterations that had been made in the roadway for years past. It was believed that the coffin and contents must have been under ground for quite 150 years.

In Cross Street, near the "Elephant and Castle," are the Drapers' Almshouses, founded by Mr. John Walter, in 1651. The houses are of brick, and were rebuilt in 1778. To these almshouses the parish has the privilege of nominating six of its own parishioners; the remainder are appointed by the Drapers' Company.

On the west side of the Kennington Road, and on the site now occupied by the horse repository, the Metropolitan Tabernacle, and the colossal block of buildings at the corner of St. George's Road, stood for many years, down till the year 1851, a picturesque cluster of almshouses belonging to the Fishmongers' Company. There were two separate buildings. One, St. Peter's Hospital, was built by the company in 1615–18; the other, due to the munificence of Mr. James Hulbert, a liveryman, dated its erection from 1719. These almshouses were quaint, old-fashioned, quadrangular piles of building, of Gothic architecture, with mullioned windows; they were enclosed by low walls, and in part surrounded by patches of garden-ground, sunk below the roadway. They appear to have been, from the first, in part supported by a voluntary appropriation, by the Company of Fishmongers, of a portion of the revenues of Sir Thomas Kneseworth's estate; but the earliest benefaction which can be considered as a specific endowment, and which seems to have given occasion to the erection of the hospital, was that by Sir Thomas Hunt, who, "by will [April 26, 1615], gave out of his land in Kent (or Kentish) Street, Southwark, £20 a year to the poor of the Company of Fishmongers, on condition that the company should build an hospital, containing houses for six poor freemen, and to have the houses rent free, and a yearly sum of 40s. a-piece, to be paid quarterly; and every of them, on St. Thomas's Day, to have a gown of three yards of good cloth, of 8s. a yard, and also 6s. in money to make it up; that if any alms-man should die, and leave a wife, so long as she should continue a widow, she should have her dwelling free, but if she should marry, she should not tarry there; and 40s. and a yearly gown should go to some honest brother of the company, who should wear the gown at times convenient, with the donor's arms on it, and the dolphin at its top."

William Hunt, Esq., son of the above-mentioned Sir Thomas, in accomplishment of his father's will, executed two several grants of annuities of £20 each, dated 16th of November, 1618, issuing from cottages and lands in Kent Street, which annuities were granted "To the governors of St. Peter's Hospital, founded by the wardens and commonalty of the Mystery of Fishmongers."

In 1616 Mr. Robert Spencer gave £50 towards erecting twelve or more almshouses for the company's poor; and in the following year, on mention of Hunt's legacy and Spencer's donation, and an estimate by the wardens that twelve dwellings could be erected for £400, the court of the company consented to the erecting thereof, "with all convenient speed;" and they obtained, on petition, from James I., dated October 2, 1618, permission to erect and establish the said almshouses, to be called "St. Peter's Hospital," and the court of the company to be incorporated by the name of "the Governors of St. Peter's Hospital, founded by the wardens and company of the Mystery of Fishmongers of the City of London," &c., with a common seal, power to hold lands, &c., and to make statutes for the government of the said hospital. The court ordered (November 23rd, 1618) that thirteen poor men and women should be placed in the hospital at the next Christmas, six of them being pursuant to Hunt's will. Each of them were to receive so much money weekly as, with the company's alms and Hunt's legacy, should make their pensions two shillings weekly.

By degrees more houses were added to those

originally built, and the whole building as it stood, down to the time of its demolition, consisting of twenty-two dwellings, a chapel, and a hall, was finished in 1636, as appeared by an inscription on the east front of the hall. The windows of the hall were enriched with painted glass, and over the chimney-piece were the arms, supporters, crest, and motto of the Fishmongers' Company. St. Peter's Hospital is now located at Wandsworth.

At the beginning of the seventeenth century there was in this parish a theatre, in which the Lord Admiral's and Lord Chamberlain's "servants" performed. This theatre was occasionally used by the players from the "Globe" at Bankside, in Shakespeare's time.* The exact site of the above-mentioned theatre is not known, but it was probably very near to the spot where now stands the "Elephant and Castle" Theatre, on the south

NEWINGTON BUTTS IN 1820.

Hulbert's Almshouses were erected on a piece of ground belonging to the Fishmongers' Company, lying on the south side of St. Peter's Hospital. It was a neat and imposing little pile, consisting of three courts with gardens behind, together with a dining-hall and chapel, and a statue of the founder on a pedestal in the centre of the enclosure.

In the high road between the "Elephant and Castle" and Kennington Park stood the old Newington Grammar School, with the date 1666 over the door, but is now removed.

There was formerly a hospital of Our Lady and St. Catherine at Newington, which continued till the year 1551, when their proctor, William Cleybrooke, being dispossessed of his home, was fortunate enough to obtain a licence to beg!

side of the New Kent Road, near the railway station.

At a short distance westward of the Fishmongers' Almshouses, near to West Square, on the south side of St. George's Road, formerly stood the tall boarded structure represented in our illustration on page 256. It served for some time the purposes of a semaphore telegraph tower.

Nearly opposite the "Elephant and Castle," and on part of the ground formerly occupied by the Fishmongers' Almshouses, stands the Metropolitan Tabernacle—better known as "Spurgeon's Chapel,"—the first stone of which was laid by Sir Samuel Morton Peto in August, 1859. The edifice, which

---

* See *ante*, p. 50.

THE METROPOLITAN TABERNACLE.

THE FISHMONGERS' ALMSHOUSES IN 1850.

is upwards of 140 feet long, 80 feet broad, and 60 feet high, is approached at the eastern end by a flight of steps which extend the whole width of the building. The principal entrances are beneath a noble portico, the entablature and pediment of which are supported by six lofty Corinthian columns. The chapel contains some 5,500 sittings of all kinds. There is room for 6,000 persons without excessive crowding; and there are also a lecture-hall capable of holding about 900, a school-room for 1,000 children, six class-rooms, "kitchen, lavatory, and retiring-rooms below stairs." Besides these the building contains "a ladies' room for working meetings, a young men's class-room, and a secretary's room on the ground floor; three vestries, for pastor, deacons, and elders on the first floor; and three store-rooms on the second floor."

As we have already had occasion to state,* the congregation for whom this edifice was erected, met originally in New Park Street Chapel, Southwark. In the month of December, 1853, Mr. Charles Haddon Spurgeon, being then nineteen years of age, preached there for the first time. It may not be out of place here to say a few words about the career of so eminent a preacher as Mr. Spurgeon. Born at Kelvedon, in Essex, in June, 1834, he was educated at Colchester, and as youth advanced he became usher in a school at Newmarket. "Some of his relatives who were Independents," as we gather from "Men of the Time," "proposed that he should enter one of their colleges, and undergo a training for the ministry. But his own convictions were in favour of other views; and accordingly he joined the church formerly presided over by the late Robert Hall, at Cambridge. From this period he became almost entirely a village preacher and tract distributor. At Teversham, a village near Cambridge, Mr. Spurgeon, under the designation of 'the Boy Preacher,' delivered his first sermon; and shortly afterwards he was invited to become pastor at a small Baptist chapel at Waterbeach. The invitation was accepted. The lad of seventeen soon became a celebrated character; the barn at Waterbeach was filled with auditors, while listening crowds contented themselves with the sound of his voice from the outside. Invitations to preach were sent to him from the surrounding places. His fame reached London; and the church at New Park Street, in Southwark, whose pulpit had in former days been occupied by Dr. Rippon, now courted his favours. This call being accepted, Mr. Spurgeon made his first appearance before a London congregation in 1853, with so much success, that ere two years had passed away it was considered necessary to enlarge the building, pending which alteration he officiated for four months at Exeter Hall; and that edifice was always so crowded, that hundreds were turned away from the doors. The enlargement of Park Street Chapel, however, proved to be insufficient. His hearers multiplied so rapidly that it became expedient to engage the Surrey Music Hall. A lamentable accident, however, having occurred within its walls in October, 1856, his followers erected for him a handsome new chapel in the Kennington Road, which was publicly opened in 1861." During the first seven years of Mr. Spurgeon's ministry in London, and in consequence of his untiring perseverance, upwards of £31,000 had been subscribed for the building, and the structure was accordingly opened free of debt.

During the short time that Mr. Spurgeon occupied the platform at Exeter Hall, paragraphs appeared in the newspapers announcing that "the Strand was blocked up by crowds who gathered to hear a young man in Exeter Hall." Remarks of no very flattering character appeared in various journals, and the multitude was thereby increased. Caricatures adorned the printsellers' windows; among them one entitled "Catch-'em-alive-O!" wherein the popular preacher was depicted with his head surmounted by one of those peculiarly-prepared sheets of fly-paper known by that name, to which were adhering or fluttering all sorts of winged characters—from the Lord Chancellor down to Mrs. Gamp—and in the most ridiculous attitudes; Mr. Spurgeon's name, too, continued to be made more and more known by pamphlets and letters in the papers, which all tended to swell the crowd. As we shall have more to say of Mr. Spurgeon and his preaching presently, when dealing with the music-hall in the Surrey Gardens, we will only add here that in treating of the hostility which the Puritans and Nonconformists have always shown to the stage, M. Alphonse Esquiros remarks in his "English at Home," that "one of the fiercest diatribes against the dramatic art was lately (1862) uttered by Mr. Spurgeon;" and he adds, "As Mr. Spurgeon is an eloquent preacher, but borrows several of his best effects from theatrical action, it has been asked whether a little professional jealousy has not been mixed up with his attacks." It would seem, however, as if there were no limits to Mr. Spurgeon's popularity, as was shown on the occasion of his 50th birthday, in 1884.

In connection with the Metropolitan Tabernacle are some almshouses and schools; a college

---

* See *ante*, p. 29.

THE PARISH CHURCH.

for training young men for the Nonconformist ministry; and an orphanage at Stockwell.

At a short distance beyond the Metropolitan Tabernacle, down to the close of the year 1875, the roadway running southward was considerably narrowed, and formed an awkward bend, by the inconvenient position of the old parish church of St. Mary, Newington, the eastern end of which closely abutted on the roadway. The extent of St. Mary's parish is thus set forth in the "New View of London" (1708):—"Beginning at the windmill near Mr. Bowyer's by Camberwell, and two fields thence westward and to Kennington Common, it extends northward from thence to Newington Church, and thence both sides of the road to the Fishmongers' Almshouses exclusive: and then on the easterly side of the way to the turning to Kent Street, with all the western side of that street to the Lock; then they pass, in walking the bounds, through Walworth Field and Common, and thence to the said windmill again: in which circuit is contained the number of 620 dwelling houses."

Not only Lysons, as we have already mentioned, but also other writers on the churches of Surrey, have stated that St. Mary's Church stood at some distance farther eastward, or have at all events expressed some difference of opinion upon the subject. Dr. H. C. Barlow, in an article in the *Builder* in May, 1874, endeavours to prove that the original site of the church—that, at least, of the Domesday Record—was where the fabric stood down to the time of its recent removal. Dr. Barlow writes:—"By means of an old document, found some years ago among my grandfather's papers—a copy of a *terrier* of the glebe lands, houses, &c., made in 1729, and of which he took a copy in 1799, when Rector's Warden—I am enabled to demonstrate that the church, since the Norman Conquest, has never changed its situation. In that portion of Domesday Book which relates to Surrey, there is a description of the manor of Waleorde (Walworth), where it is said there is a church with eight acres of meadow-land. The first mention of Neweton (Newington) occurs in the Testa de Nevil (*sive Liber Feodorum* in *Curia Saccarii*), of the time of Henry III., or the first half of the thirteenth century; it is there stated that the queen's goldsmith holds of the king, *in capite*, one acre of land in Neweton, by the service of rendering a gallon of honey. In the taxation of spiritualities made by Pope Nicholas IV., in 1292, the church is spoken of as being at Newington; and in the Archbishop of Canterbury's Register, 1313, the parish is called Newington *juxta* London.

"The living was a rectory, then in the archbishop's gift, and of increasing value. In the time of King Edward the Confessor it was worth only xxx. *solidi*, but when the Domesday Survey was made it was worth double that sum. The manor, on the contrary, was becoming of less importance. The first notice we have of it is that Edmund Ironside gave it to Hitard, his jester, who, on going to Rome, gave it to Christ Church, Canterbury. In King Edward's time it was taxed for five hides (500 acres), but at the time of the survey, for three hides and a half only, nearly one-third less. After the thirteenth century we hear no more of the church at Walworde; from that time the church is said to be at Newington. The question, therefore, is, did the original church stand at Walworth, and was subsequently moved to Newington, or did it only change its name with the new name given to the parish? Lysons, who wrote, in 1791, 'Environs of London,' suggests that the church might have been rebuilt on a new site, and becoming surrounded by houses, the locality received the name of Neweton, or Newtown, subsequently Newington. But this suggestion is a mere hypothesis. Where churches have been first built there is a general disposition on the part of ecclesiastics to retain them; the pious urn commonly desire to worship God where their forefathers knelt before them, and it is the duty of the clergy to encourage this sentiment. In those days there were no London improvements required at Newington to endanger the sacred fabric and change its hallowed locality. When churches need rebuilding, it has been the rule in England to rebuild them where they stood before, and I shall be able to show that the church at Walworde, otherwise Newington, was no exception to this laudable practice.

"The words of Domesday record are—'*Ibi Ecclesia et* viii. *acræ prati.*' These eight acres of meadow-land were attached to the church, and formed the church field. They were also contiguous to the manor, which was of large extent, and in King Edward's time, consisting of 500 acres, occupied nearly the whole of the present parish, which contains only 630 acres, including Walworth Common. Even the 350 acres, the extent of the manor at the time of the Conquest, supposing the present manor-house to stand near the site of the original one, and to indicate the probable centre of the manor, would bring the situation of Newington Church within the full meaning of the words '*Ibi Ecclesia et* viii. *acræ prati.*' The old church at Newington had a low square tower of flint and rag-stone, similar to other church towers in Surrey that date from the fourteenth century, or somewhat earlier, and its becoming surrounded with houses was comparatively a recent event.

"Manning and Bray, in their great history of Surrey, have no hesitation in considering Waleorde (Walworth), still the name of the manor, to be the same as Newington; and the Rev. Mr. Hussey, in his account of the churches in Surrey, remarks, if this be so, then the Domesday church was at Newington, not at Walworth. The Domesday church was where the eight acres of meadow-land were, and these were at Newington.

"Among the items contained in the *terrier* of the glebe lands, &c., made in 1729, when the Rev. Wm. Taswell was rector, is one which begins as follows:—'*Item.* On the south side of the churchyard there lies a parcel of pasture and meadow ground, called the church-field, in the occupation of the Widow Harwood, containing about seven and a-half acres. This church-field formerly contained eight acres, but in the year 1648, part of it, containing in length about two hundred yards, and in breadth about four yards, was taken out of it to make a footway leading from Newington to the east end of Kinnington Lane; and in the year 1718, the trustees for mending and repairing the road from Newington to Vauxhall took about fourteen feet in breadth, and about forty-eight feet in length, from the church-field aforesaid, to widen the road turning from Newington to Kinnington, which road was before so narrow, that two waggons could not meet there. . . . .'

"The *terrier* also states that two small pieces of the church-field were taken, one about 1637, and the other in 1665, to enlarge the churchyard. There can be no manner of doubt, therefore, but that the church, with its eight acres of meadow-land, recorded in 'Domesday Book,' was one and the same with the church at Newington, and that we may say of the latter, as the record says of the former, '*Ibi Ecclesia et* viii. *acræ prati*,' though it would now be impossible to find any portion of the latter which has not been brought into subjection under the despotic law of the spread of bricks and mortar."

The old parish church of Newington appears to have been, in earlier days, a very small and insignificant structure; Sir Hugh Brawne added a north aisle about the year 1600. In the early part of the last century several hundred pounds were expended in repairing and "ornamenting" the fabric; but this was all to very little purpose, for in a few years it was found necessary that the whole building, except the tower, should be taken down. The new church, on the same inconvenient spot, by the side of a great road, was opened in March, 1721. Being found inadequate to the increased number of inhabitants, an Act of Parliament was obtained in 1790 for rebuilding the church upon a larger scale. The work of reconstruction was commenced in the following year, and completed in about two years. The unsightly structure was constructed of brick, with a portico in the west front, and on the roof was a small bell-turret.

FOUNTAIN IN THE SURREY GARDENS.

In this church, according to Manning and Bray's "History of Surrey," was buried a certain facetious individual, Mr. Serjeant Davy, who died in 1780, and of whom a good story is told. He was originally a chemist at Exeter; and a sheriff's officer coming to serve on him a process from the Court of Common Pleas, he civilly asked him if he would not take something to drink. While the man was leisurely quenching his thirst Davy contrived to heat the poker, and then told the bailiff that if he did not eat the writ, which was of sheepskin, he should be made to swallow the poker. The officer very naturally preferred the parchment; but the Court of Common Pleas, not being then accustomed to Davy's jokes, sent him an order to appear at Westminster Hall, and committed him to the Fleet Prison for contempt. From this strange circumstance he acquired his first taste for the law. On his discharge from prison he applied himself to the study of it in earnest, was called to the bar, obtained the coif, and enjoyed a good practice for many years.

Here, too, was buried Thomas Middleton, author of the *Mask of Cupid; A Mad World, my Masters;* the *Spanish Gipsy; Anything for a Quiet Life,* and very many other comedies, besides sundry less well-known tragedies. He died in July, 1627; and his widow, who followed him to the grave next year, was buried at the expense of the Corporation of London, who had employed her husband to write the *Mask of Cupid,* performed with other "solemnities" at Merchant Taylors' Hall, to commemorate the marriage of the infamous Earl and Countess of Somerset.

On the floor of the old church was, among others, the grave-stone of George Powell, who is said, by the editor of "Aubrey's Perambulations of Surrey," to have been styled " King of the Gipsies," and to have died in the year 1704, in very flourishing circumstances—in fact, as rich, or rather as poor, as a king.

The churchyard, which was enlarged by Act of Parliament in the reign of George II., contains among its numerous monuments one to the memory of William Allen, a young man who was killed by the firing of the soldiers in the riots which took place in St. George's Fields, in 1768, on the occasion of the confinement of John Wilkes in the King's Bench Prison; around the monument are several inscriptions expressing strong political feelings.

"The most eminent ecclesiastic who ever held this rectory," writes Thomas Allen, in his "History of Surrey," "was Dr. Samuel Horsley, who was presented to it in 1759. This eminent character was born in the parish of St. Martin-in-the-Fields, in October, 1733. He was educated at Westminster School, and Trinity Hall, Cambridge, where he took the degree of LL.B. In 1767 he was chosen a Fellow of the Royal Society, and he soon after published some elaborate treatises. In 1768 he took the degree of LL.D., and in 1773 he was elected secretary to the Royal Society, and not long after the Earl of Aylesford presented him to the rectory of Aldbury, in this county. About 1784 Dr. Horsley withdrew from the Royal Society, and about the same period commenced a literary conference with the great champion of Unitarianism, Dr. Priestley. The talent and energy with which he exerted himself called forth the approbation of Lord Chancellor Thurlow, who characteristically remarked that 'those who defended the Church ought to be supported by the Church,' and accordingly presented him to a prebendal stall in Gloucester Cathedral, and shortly after he was made Bishop of St. David's. In his episcopal character he supported the reputation for learning and ability which he had previously acquired. In Parliament he was the strenuous advocate for the existing state of things in religion and politics; and the merit of his conduct will accordingly be differently appreciated with reference to the various opinions of different persons. His zeal did not go unrewarded, for he was presented to the see of Rochester in 1793, and made Dean of Westminster; and in 1802 he was translated to St. Asaph. He died at Brighton, October 4, 1806, and was interred in St. Mary's Church, Newington."

In this church was baptised, about the year 1810, George Alexander Gratton, a spotted negro boy, who was shown about London and the provinces as a curiosity by Richardson. He died when only five years old, in February, 1813, and was buried at Great Marlow, where there is a monument to his memory.

In 1871, it was proposed by the Board of Works, under the Metropolitan Improvements Act, to have the church removed, with the view of widening the roadway at that point, and an offer of £5,000 was made by the Board for that special purpose. In 1875 a grant of £4,000 was obtained from the London Churches Fund, and a subscription, headed by the rector with £1,000, was opened among the parishioners for the remainder of the money required, about £9,000. A site for a new church was obtained from the Ecclesiastical Commissioners, in a more central part of the parish, on the east side of the Kennington Park Road. This church, a large and lofty Gothic edifice of stone, having been completed, with the exception of the tower, the demolition of the old church was forthwith commenced. In 1876 the materials of the old edifice were disposed of by public auction, and realised a sum of £538. The remains of some five hundred persons were carefully removed from the churchyard, and re-interred in a vault built for the purpose. In one instance two bodies were taken from under the altar, and the inscriptions on the coffins showed that they were the remains of Dr. Horsley and his wife, the latter of whom died in 1805. The remains were in a state of preservation, having been buried some fifteen feet below the surface. They were removed to Thorley, in Herts, by the family of the deceased bishop. Among the other remains which were disinterred there was the skeleton of a man who had been buried in a complete suit of black, the coat and boots being perfect.

Besides the old church several houses in the High Street close by were demolished at the same time, and the graveyard, thus curtailed by the widening of the road, was set in order and opened to the public as a garden. The whole is enclosed by some neat iron railings and gates; and a handsome Gothic clock-tower has been erected on the site of the church. This tower is fourteen feet square at the base, and carried up in five stages with buttresses to a height of about a hundred feet. The clock-face is placed at the height of seventy feet. In the lower part of the building the material is Portland stone, the remainder being of Bath stone, and the front to Newington Butts, as well as the two sides, is enriched with carvings in florid Gothic. There is a doorway in the centre of the front, with windows in the upper part. On the left side of the doorway is the following inscription:—"This tower was built at the expense of Robert Faulconer, Esq., Anno Domini 1877, on the site of the old parish church of St. Mary's, Newington." This handsome gift, which has the great advantage of a position in which it can be well seen, cost the donor £5,000.

The old parsonage-house, which stood in the rear of the church and of Mr. Spurgeon's "Tabernacle," and which was reputed to date from the sixteenth century, was built of wood, and surrounded at one time by a moat, over which were several bridges. The land in the immediate neighbourhood was formerly intersected by numerous ditches, some of which existed till quite recent times. They ran in various directions, completely surrounding the rectory grounds. To reach the "Queen's Head" tea-gardens, which occupied the site of the present National Schoolroom, it was necessary to cross some of these ditches by a small wooden bridge. The tea-gardens were in a line with Temple Street, at the western end of the Metropolitan Tabernacle. Indeed, so well watered was the neighbourhood of Newington Butts, that, if we may believe tradition, in 1571 occurred a great flood, so that the people were obliged to be conveyed in boats from the church "to the pinfolds, near St. George's, in Southwark."

Among the residents of Newington in the middle of the last century, was James Short, an eminent

OLD NEWINGTON CHURCH IN 1866.

optician, and a native of Edinburgh. He enjoyed a high reputation in his day for the excellence of his reflecting telescopes, of the Gregorian kind, by the sale of which he amassed a large fortune. He died at Newington in 1768.

On the east side of Kennington Park Road, and soon after obtained possession of the grounds formerly attached to the 'Manor House' at Walworth. The grounds comprised in all about fifteen acres, which were utilised to their fullest extent, exclusive of a sheet of water covering nearly three acres more. The gardens were approached from

THE MUSIC HALL, SURREY GARDENS, 1858.

Manor Place, Walworth, and there was a second entrance from Penton Place, Kennington Road. The large conservatory, three hundred feet in circumference, and containing upwards of 6,000 feet of glass, was at that time the largest building of its kind in England. This was afterwards used to enclose the cages of the lions, tigers, and other carnivora. In the year 1834 was exhibited here a one-horned Indian rhinoceros, for which Cross paid £800; two years later three giraffes were added to his collection. The first picture was 'Mount Vesuvius,' painted by Danson, in 1837, the lake representing the Bay of Naples, and a display of fireworks serving vividly to illustrate the eruption, which was nightly repeated in the presence of admiring crowds, and served as the chief attraction of the place for upwards of two years. Then followed, in 1839, a representation of 'Iceland and Mount Hecla;' in 1841, the 'City of Rome,'

near the junction of that thoroughfare with Kennington Lane and Newington Butts, is Penton Place, through which is one of the approaches to the Surrey Gardens, formerly known as the Surrey Zoological Gardens. This place of entertainment, which has undergone many vicissitudes, is thus described by a writer in the *Era* Almanack for 1871:—

"When Exeter Change ceased to exist, the then proprietor, Mr. Edward Cross, removed his menagerie to the King's Mews at Charing Cross, which occupied five acres, and was painted on a surface upwards of 250,000 feet square; in 1843, the 'Temple of Ellora;' in 1844, 'London during the Great Fire of 1666;' in 1845, the 'City of Edinburgh.' In 1846 'Vesuvius' was reproduced; in 1848 there was a revival of 'Rome;' in 1849 there was the 'Storming of Badajoz,' with 'new effects of real ordnance.' In this same year M. Jullien organised a series of promenade concerts on four evenings in each week, the admission remaining fixed, as before, at a shilling. The fireworks were always a great attraction of the gardens. In 1850 was exhibited 'Napoleon's Passage over the Alps;' in this picture were represented some fifty thousand men in motion, who, in the front, appeared of life-size, and who, in fact, were living men, but who were made, by an optical illusion, to dwindle gradually at different distances to the veriest specks which the eye could track along the zigzag line of ascent towards the summit of the Alpine Pass, where stood the monastery of St. Bernard, ready to receive the weary and half-frozen troops and their imperial master. On the death of Mr. Cross the proprietorship and management of the gardens devolved on his secretary and assistant, a man named Tyler, who conducted them for some years, when the property became vested in a Limited Liability Company. In 1856 the gardens were put up to auction, and the Surrey Music Hall was erected upon a portion of the grounds. The gardens were used in 1856 for the purpose of entertaining the Guards with a public dinner after their return from the Crimea; and again, in 1862, they were re-opened with a picture of the 'City and Bay of Naples,' showing Vesuvius in the distance. But the fitful taste of the public did not care for the revival; and though a variety of fresh amusements in succession was announced and provided, yet it was found that the place had lost its popularity to a degree which was irretrievable, and accordingly the gardens were closed. The grounds were afterwards more advantageously occupied, as the temporary Hospital of St. Thomas, before its removal to Lambeth Walk."

The principal walks and avenues were planted with every description of native and exotic forest trees that would endure the climate; whilst the beautiful sheet of water, mentioned above, was spotted with islands, shrubberies, and plantations of great richness. Numerous rustic-looking buildings, with thatched roofs, were to be seen in different parts, each of them adding to the picturesqueness of the grounds. Mr. Loudon, the editor of the *Gardeners' Magazine*, thus speaks of the buildings these gardens at the time of their opening:—

"The London Zoological Society has certainly the merit of taking the lead in this description of garden; but Mr. Cross has not only proceeded more rapidly than they have done, but has erected more suitable and more imposing structures than are yet to be found in the gardens in the Regent's Park. What is there, for example, in the latter garden which can be at all compared with the circular glass building 300 feet in diameter, combining a series of examples of tropical quadrupeds and birds, and of exotic plants? In the plan of this building the animals (lions, tigers, leopards, &c.) are kept in separate cages or compartments towards the centre; exterior to them is a colonnade, supporting the glazed roof, and also for cages of birds; within this colonnade will be placed hot-water pipes for heating the whole, and beyond it is an open paved area for spectators; next, there is a channel for a stream of water, intended for gold, silver, and other exotic fishes; and, beyond, a border, under the front wall, for climbing plants, to be trained on wires under the roof."

The grounds were laid out under the superintendence of Mr. Henry Phillips, the author of "Sylva Florifera," and it is almost impossible to give the reader an idea of their beauty and variety. Besides the large glass building mentioned above, there were several movable aviaries and cages for the feathered tribes; whilst one of the prettiest spots was the "beaver-dam," a small pond partly enclosed by rockwork. Altogether, at one time these gardens offered a great rival attraction to those at the Regent's Park, which we have already described.* In 1834 a live female gorilla was added to this menagerie, and proved a great favourite of the visitors. The collection here was not so extensive as that in the Regent's Park, but some of the animals were much finer, particularly one of the lions.

A story—we fear rather apocryphal—is told of one of the lions here in the early part of their existence. A small black spaniel being thrown into his cage, instead of killing and eating it, the king of beasts took it under his protection, fondled it, and played with it; and when it died, the lion was so deeply grieved that he survived the loss of his companion only a few days!

The volcanic exhibitions at the Surrey Zoological Gardens probably had their origin in the Ranelagh spectacles of the last century; for in 1792 was shown in the latter gardens a beautiful representation of Mount Etna, with the flowing of the lava

---

* See Vol. V., p. 282.

down its sides. The height of the boarded work which represented the mountain was about eighty feet, and the whole exhibited a curious specimen of machinery and pyrotechnics. Of the Surrey Gardens, as they existed in the year of grace 1850, Mr. H. Mayhew wrote, "Mount Etna, the fashionable volcano of the season, just now is vomiting here its sky-rockets and Roman candles."

During the last few years of their existence, these gardens added the attractions of music. A large covered orchestra, capable of accommodating a large number of performers, was fitted up on the margin of the lake, for the purpose of giving open-air concerts on a gigantic scale; and this was retained during the summer months by Jullien's band. Jullien led the orchestra at the concerts here in 1851, the year of the Great Exhibition.

The Surrey Music Hall, mentioned above—a large oblong building—is admirably adapted for the purposes for which it was built. At each corner are octagonal towers containing staircases, originally crowned by ornamental turrets. An arcade surrounds the ground-floor, whilst to the first and second floors are external galleries covered by verandas. The great hall, which holds 12,000 persons, exclusive of the orchestra, cost upwards of £18,000. It is twenty feet longer and thirty feet wider than the Great Room at Exeter Hall.

On Sundays it was used temporarily for the religious services held by Mr. C. H. Spurgeon, on his first sudden rush into popularity in London; and on the first occasion of holding these services, —the evening of October 19, 1856—it was the scene of a serious and fatal accident, seven persons being killed by a false alarm of fire raised by some reckless and wanton jesters. We have already spoken of Mr. Spurgeon in our account of the Metropolitan Tabernacle, but we may further remark here that, notwithstanding the above-mentioned occurrence, large numbers continued for the space of three years to hear Mr. Spurgeon on Sunday mornings. A letter, signed "*Habitans in Sicco*," and dated from "Broad Phylactery, West-

VIEW IN THE SURREY GARDENS, 1850.

minster," appeared at this period in the *Times;* part of it ran as follows:—"'I want to hear Spurgeon; let us go.' Now, I am supposed to be a High Churchman, so I answered, 'What! go and hear a Calvinist—a Baptist!—a man who ought to be ashamed of himself for being so near the Church, and yet not within its pale?' 'Never mind; come and hear him.' Well, we went yesterday morning to the Music Hall, in the Surrey Gardens. . . . Fancy a congregation consisting of 10,000 souls, streaming into the hall, mounting the galleries, humming, buzzing, and swarming—a mighty hive of bees—eager to secure at first the best places, and, at last, any place at all. After waiting more than half an hour—for if you wish to have a seat you must be there at least that space of time in advance—Mr.

Spurgeon ascended his tribune. To the hum, and rush, and trampling of men, succeeded a low, concentrated thrill and murmur of devotion, which seemed to run at once, like an electric current, through the breast of every one present, and by this magnetic chain the preacher held us fast bound for about two hours. It is not my purpose to give a summary of his discourse. It is enough to say of his voice, that its power and volume are sufficient to reach every one in that vast assembly; of his language, that it is neither high-flown nor homely; of his style, that it is at times familiar, at times declamatory, but always happy, and often eloquent; of his doctrine, that neither the 'Calvinist' nor the 'Baptist' appears in the forefront of the battle which is waged by Mr. Spurgeon with relentless animosity, and with Gospel weapons, against irreligion, cant, hypocrisy, pride, and those secret bosom-sins which so easily beset a man in daily life; and to sum up all in a word, it is enough to say of the man himself, that he impresses you with a perfect conviction of his sincerity. But I have not written so much about my children's want of spiritual food when they listened to the mumbling of the Archbishop of ———, and my own banquet at the Surrey Gardens, without a desire to draw a practical conclusion from these two stories, and to point them by a moral. Here is a man not more Calvinistic than many an incumbent of the Established Church who 'humbles and mumbles,' as old Latimer says, over his liturgy and text—here is a man who says the complete immersion, or something of the kind, of adults, is necessary to baptism. These are his faults of doctrine; but if I were the examining chaplain of the Archbishop of ———, I would say, 'May it please your grace, here is a man able to preach eloquently, able to fill the largest church in England with his voice, and, what is more to the purpose, with people. And may it please your grace, here are two churches in the metropolis, St. Paul's and Westminster Abbey. What does your grace think of inviting Mr. Spurgeon, this heretical Calvinist and Baptist, who is able to draw 10,000 souls after him, just to try his voice, some Sunday morning, in the nave of either of those churches?'"

In June, 1861, shortly after being vacated by Mr. Spurgeon, the Music Hall was destroyed by fire. It was, however, rebuilt, and for a time was occupied as a temporary hospital during the demolition of St. Thomas's Hospital at London Bridge and the erection of the new building near Westminster Bridge.

The old Manor House of Walworth is kept in remembrance by Manor Road and Manor Place, the last-named thoroughfare uniting Penton Place with Walworth Road. Close by, in Penrose Street, is a commodious lecture-hall, built in 1862, under the auspices of the Walworth Mechanics' Institute. This institution was founded in 1845, in Manor Place, and is the only literary and scientific institution on a large scale on the south side of the Thames; the library contains some 5,000 volumes, and it has a reading-room in the Walworth Road.

Since the commencement of the present century a considerable advance has been made in the way of buildings in this neighbourhood, particularly on the east side of the Walworth Road. Lock's Fields, formerly a dreary swamp, and Walworth Common, which was at one time an open field, have been covered with houses. In Paragon Row the Fishmongers' Company have erected several model dwellings, with the aim of benefiting a very poor locality. The dwellings have been built on the "flat" system, realising as nearly as possible the idea of the cottage character, and replacing old and dilapidated houses of an inferior class.

Whatever this locality may be in the present day, it has not been without its places of amusement in former times, for we learn from Colburn's "Kalendar of Amusements" for 1840, that the Marylebone and Oxford cricket clubs played a match in that year at the "Beehive" grounds, Walworth.

In 1823 the first stone of St. Peter's Church, Walworth, was laid by the Archbishop of Canterbury, immediately after the performance of the like ceremony at Trinity Church, in this parish.[*] The church, which is situated at a short distance on the eastern side of the Walworth Road, is built of brick, with the exception of the steeple and architectural ornaments, which are constructed of stone. The basement is occupied by spacious catacombs.

St. John's Church, which stands a short distance backward on the eastern side of the Walworth Road, near York Street, is a lofty and handsome Gothic building, in the Decorated style, and was erected in 1865, at a cost of upwards of £5,000. It was endowed by the Dean and Chapter of Canterbury, who are the patrons.

Walworth is not entirely devoid of historical memorabilia, if tradition is to be trusted; a native of this village—for such it must have been in his day—was William Walworth, the celebrated Lord Mayor of London, who slew Wat Tyler with his own hand, and who, in memory of the deed, caused a dagger to be added to the arms of the City.

---

[*] See *ante*, p. 253.